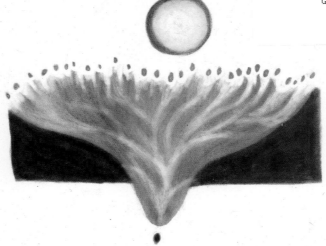

one night, an elephant

a book of poems and pictures

by

Seth Randall-Goddard
&
Kit Perceval

All Around Publishing

First published by All Around Publishing in 2021
www.allaroundpublishing.co.uk

ISBN 978-1-8381156-2-3

Book design by Kitty Perceval
Printed by Ex Why Zed

To Chris, Dotty, Pia,
who continually inspire me to
do more.
-Seth

To Rosie and Eds, whom I love
very much.
-Kit

The City

Mangoes In Edinburgh

It was raining: the drops hung flat and metallic,
Thrown across Edinburgh's streets
So that not even the awnings of highstreet vendors
Or stern umbrellas held by suits
Could help us —
We decided to duck into the nearby churchyard
(St Cuthbert's Kirk I think it was)
To wait it out.
The graves, rank upon rank,
Stood like knuckles across the waking grass;
Rain hit so hard it made a dewy mist.

My friend and I were drawn to one stone
Squatting there, black like lead;
Two flanking skulls proclaimed
"Remember Death!
Here Lies the Corps of
Elizabeth Bellfridge
Spouse to George Allan Messenger".

These skulls were not proud,
They were plain.
A craftsperson duly knocked them out.
Duty rang with hammer to stone,
The body long since gone.

Nowadays we have swept aside death and decay,
We ignore it.
The smells themselves have gone;
Our flowers are plastic.
They will outlive us all a thousand times.

We stood and walked around again,
Then left those crumbling monoliths,
Finding those parts of the city held
In agitation and deepest sighs —
You know the parts — the bits that crumble still
So when you reach out, you grasp and
Cut your palms, trip and
Bruise yourself on pebbledash walls.
It felt, at least, like something.

We know what's planned
Is worse: the golden lustre of a
Showhome balcony,
Back entrances for the cleaner,
Balconies so high they split the sun
And crack open the moon
And what rains out is evergreen
Palm trees and mangoes on the concrete
Lain over by tarmac and more mangoes

Which are also made of plastic.

Old Flats

Standing on the rooftop of
Our old, rented flat
In Elephant and Castle
We watched the skyline.
It was clearer then
(As now it isn't),
Feeding pigeons
porridge from a spoon found in a
Dorset Junk shop.
It was cold; the light,
though patchy,
Was still plentiful
(As now it isn't),
Like someone had scattered
Seeds & the ground had sprouted
Plastic, concrete, fibreglass
Towers
Towers that cast shadows
On our old, rented flat.

Nobody real lives there
I said
& yet somehow, as the towers went up
The streets around them emptied.
Where did all those people go?

There are fewer people now;
Different people, smooth and fresh
Plucked from catalogues,
Standing high in turrets of glass
And plastic that will never rot,
As they will never rot.
Standing on the balcony
Of our old, rented flat,
I drew a breath
The air was cold —
Again I drew a breath —
The light was dimmed,
But the panes of these towers were clear.

In this catalogue world
The streets are always clear.

Cast Iron Ravens

Two ravens stood here once.
They were cast in iron
& glowered & loomed so
Each entrant to my blue-black door was forced
To stoop to pass them by.
Protecting something lost to time,
They sunk in coadestone, cheap furniture, lime
Kilns, across the canal in Peckham.
But perhaps I'm muddling things…
134 years is a long time to frown.

Certainly the ravens stood here
Until a decade ago
When, in the dead of night —
To feed a family
To get rich quick
To buy some bread
To pay the rent — they went;
A saw was heard biting into brick.

That night, the stars were sparks and iron filings.

Liverpool Street Station

With fake rust resting over temporary monuments
To Spitalfields market— statues in front of chic,
New shopfronts selling
Some washed-out notion of history,
Bland and soft,
With notions of progress; onward march!
Ten bronze men in a bronze boat, a copper goat,
Not even stuck into the pavement,
They're just resting there. By tomorrow they'll
Be moved along
So hurry up, catch a glimpse —
Any more dawdling
And not spending money
You'll miss your train.
But look again;
The statues glossy in the rain,
There's a grey man
Lying dead by his bike
With shopping bags piled high
& then you look closer
(But don't get closer)
To see that he's actually still breathing,
Enough so you can still make your train
If he doesn't wake up.
It only really matters, you realise,
Because it's meant to be like this.

Maybe he wasn't supposed to die
But it acts as ample warning
To the labour-force; the unhoused are there
In your place
So be grateful
You still get to see the moon
Half-gassed by fume though it is.
You still get burnt by the sun.
Make no mistake:
Those empty glossy shopfronts
Look better without people.

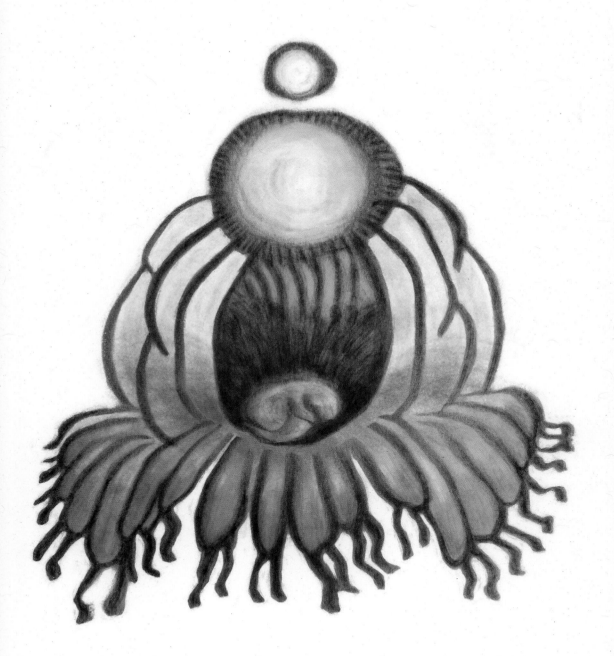

The Village Elders

Up & down my street
Which I have returned to again & again
This time for sickness, in other times for health,
Three men, three women,
Haunt the paving stones.
Once upon a time they
Tended to the gripes & convalescence
Of the street.

I know how fragile a memory can be
When shown to the light,
Like when my mother found
Bags of sugar from The War
In her basement,
Black market trade stuffed under floorboards,
Piled like sandbags.
The disturbance of the torchlight
Caused the hessian sacks to blister
& crumble,
Return to the past
That they refused to be left behind in.
The sweetness survives in the sugared pills
That also lodge themselves in memory
Given to me as a child by my mother,
Advised by the three wise women & the three
Grand men
Who governed like one implacable oak
Communicating across space & time.

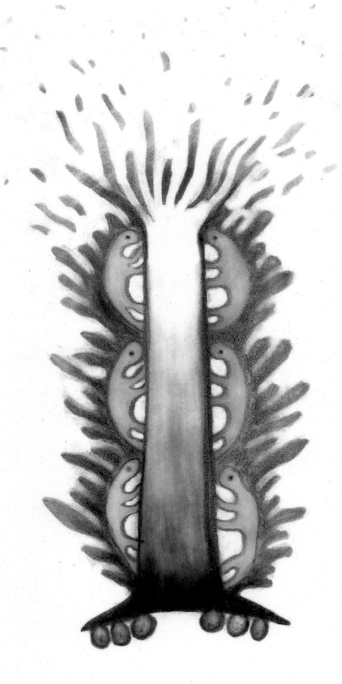

Three Pears

Sat cold in a tenement block in Glasgow, just off
Sauchiehall street, my friend took the soft brown bag
Of pears
Which I had picked, all three,
From the floor of the market
Just by the great, green river
And made jam by them.
The pears bubbled. Crystals bloomed
And fused, melting as the
Snow fell onto the windowpane.

Back in London, a week passed;
I heard no more of them.
The days darkened imperceptibly.
I squirrelled away into my very long flat,
With its very thick walls — then one day
I was sent them by post,
Those pears wrapped in brown paper packaging,
Pears which I had picked from the floor
Of the market
Just by the great, green river.
"For your birthday"
Was her note.

Alone, I spread the jam,
Brown like tudor mud,
On toast.
It burnt my tongue.
My breath came out
Like crisp white linen.

As I stared out at the
Great, green river,
I felt that one day it would rise —
That river —
Would rise and flood the floor of the market.
All the fruit
would scatter.
Those pears would rise too
Follow the stained city streets
To the river once again.
The price tags would dissolve and fall
From the greengrocer's stalls
The supermarkets and checkout tills
Would collapse, and be no more
And those pears,
In their brown paper packaging,
Would surely find the sea

Back to you.

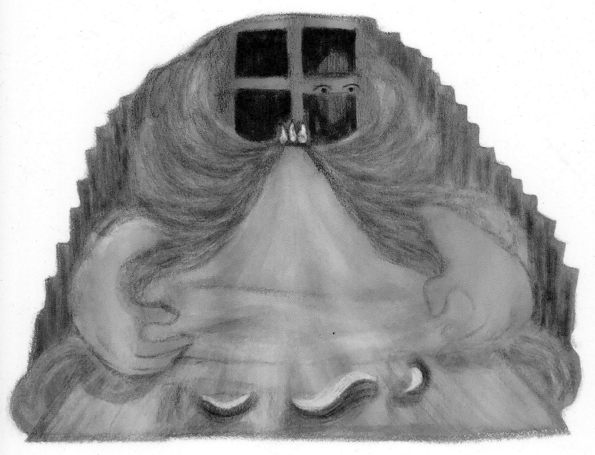

Connecting

Sailor's Trousers

Blue felt coat
Fringed with gold
She wore in a Belgian Cafe.
I saw it first, before I saw her,
Cut like a paper pattern.
If I hadn't been eating a burger like an oaf
I'd have said hello

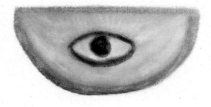

And what did you eat, last week in Brussels?

… Lamb's hearts cut with
Scissors into four
& speared on a knife.
Was greedy over giant
Wet clods of beef;
Waiters grinned & scraped & bowed,
Watching whilst I tore into the warm fat
Of a piece of wobbling pink
Ham. I paid for none of
It then, though my body would later.
My host egged me on.
"Your palate must be grown,"
He said, "& in Brussels we eat meat, meat, meat!"

It piled higher & higher
In heavy ceramic bowls -
The thick & drowsy heat obscured
The deprivation outside -
Whilst three full trays of silver & rump
Staked its claim on my soul.
What I longed for was simply this -
The tartness of a lemon,
The sweetness of an orange,
Fumbling off the skin in my pocket
As I walk away.

17

Pond Scum

To sit by the edge of the pond
& be told your face is older now,
& when we kissed I loved you,
& when we kissed you didn't love me,
But those geese beside us once were raptors
Picked up by fate & cosmic rock
Look at the way they chew the grass,
The motion of their feathers
Heated by the dying sun.
Ripples like the grey-green pool
We see beyond.

And so we sat; passed the joint
Side-to-side, hand on hand,
Surrounded by duck & gale
Tied by our reluctance to each other
To the earth beneath us.

Growing

Flying from a party near Heathrow,
Skidding along the night
In matching steel bicycles
Kicking up mud and grit and rain
We found the canal —
Your boat rocked softly.

The wind lashed against us,
Jealous at the warmth we held inside.
We knew this had happened before,
Though not in this life, nor these bodies —
As you took out a book of Federici
& read me slim paragraphs
About 600-year-old fences and mulberry bushes,
A world of borders.

The tungsten light drew in, shallow,
Our breath misted the plexiglass windows,
Where we drew circles
To see the broiling tide.
An alder tapped its branch
Staccato, our shaking fingers
Tracing the sentences,
As we found ourselves
Alone at last.

Sewage Plains

The beach by the sewage refinery works
In Lincolnshire
Was soft and flat.
Imagine — the tide was out, lapping at the edges
Of the sand: a blank piece of paper.
On this we stood,
Leaning into the wind
Like our bodies were driftwood and old tools,
Pinned together
With mudlarks' nails and butterfly pins.

Those days were long and good.
Our hands were never idle.
I've heard you wake now
To a wide, ochre plain.
Long shadows, burnt into the soil,
Stretch their fingertips from distant mountains
of dust built on dust,
& reaching your face, sullenly withdraw,
Leaving you brightened by the southern morn.

Ash handled hammer,
You go, building your nest where you may,
Following where the rivers lead,
Where the wind bears you, and you lay,
Light pouring through your sycamore limbs.
My friend, you became the wood,
That hopeful driftwood,
With all its lightness
And saintly purpose.

I fear that all I became
Was the rust.

Alive Again

We lay in your bed, hesitant;
It felt more like the Great North Wood,
Pierced by grass stalks, root heads,
Peckham rye grains & with
A moon like a punched silver disc.

I was surprised it didn't wobble in the storm
(In the wind that pitched against
The window) and was glad
When you made up your mind;
Pulling the covers back,
We lay
As all the torment outside grew.

The pigeons on the balcony outside
Huddled beak to each others' wing,
Hidden from the plastic bags & muck whipped up
From London's secret stash
Of pornography & grief,
& broken umbrellas
That once resisted rain, and now bowing,
Resisted each drop no more,
As we resisted no more,
Sinking willingly into the river.

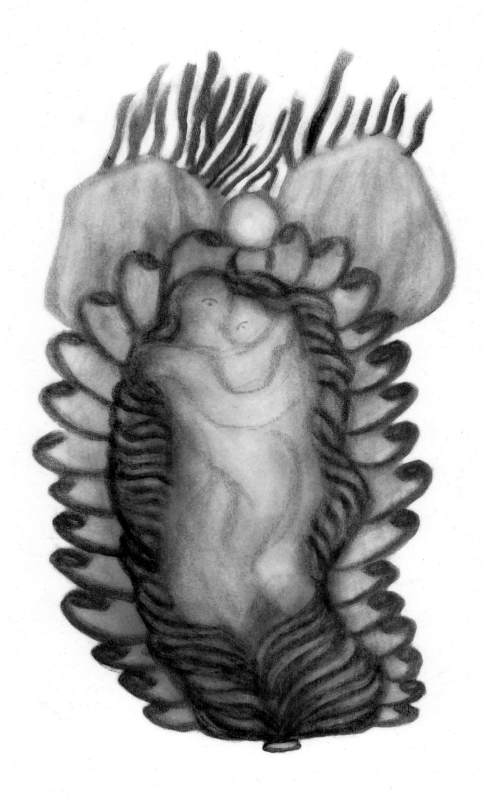

Hampstead Coffee

Even the rain drops seem impatient
As they dash & shoot & winnow,
Hampering sight as we stare out of this old shop window
Cleaned each Friday, 11AM on the dot
For the past sixty years.

The view extends twelve feet ahead
Through tall windows for plastic buildings that stand
Where fields once lay
& rivers, foundered on clay beds
& cesspits, of ancient pottery and shit
All looked up to the inky plumage of the sky
Where, still, Venus lies
For whom polyphonic singers of bronze, aged
From youth to eternity
Sang and danced for ten thousand years
Till they were silenced
& that arcing sky was blinded.

We still look up to it,
seeing less than those who came before,
As we stumble joyful and aching
From the tinted glass of London clubs
Or rise early,
Cloth and broom in hand,
To see dawn rise on Hampstead Heath
& clean the avenues of the rich
Or make them coffee
(Burn their sap milk till our fingers ring
themselves in pain
& fury.)

We crane our necks skyward.
Still the impatient rain looks down
Filling the moment before the next;
Maybe Derek Jarman saw those stars
Perhaps he scrambled in those same bushes
Fucking under trees;
Perhaps a rosebush gave him a prick.
Those nights were as long as the days
We now face,
Each moment
Washed away by that very same rain.

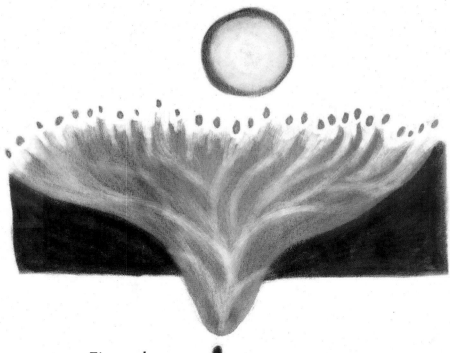

Fireworks

The fireworks, it seemed, were as eager to
Disappear as I was.
Up they went in the warm, winter sky
& fizzled away — gone, with hardly a bang.
To tell the truth
I wanted gone, too.
Not that I wasn't having a nice time —
Quite the opposite.
But sometimes
In the dusty heat of the darkness
Comes an irrepressible urge to shed
This single body and feel the wholeness
Of life that comes with
Nothingness — of death, or a sort of particular
Flatness, being spatially decentred,
Seeing the image of the moon and not being able
To touch it.

In these moments
I could care less about new boots,
Buying a house in the Cotswolds,
A romance novel I could barely relate to —
Half-heard impressions of words and
Not the words themselves.
Having come so far to stare at the sky
I groaned
& nobody heard me amidst all the other
Sounds.

Family

Hollywood, You Kill Me

Hand round the black handle
Of the kettle
As it shuddered & bucked —
Vapour steamed, covered the thin
Spindle-sticks of ply
Gripped tight in the palms
Of my brother and I.
In them we saw bent hulls of ships, carracks
& caravels, long spit-strings of rigging
Like drool, with rudders yet uncarved —
But all the size of mice!

Our grandfather sailed steel ships,
Built wooden models for museums
By & large they've all been wrecked
In dusty containers made of tin
Or, nameless, locked in cabinets
Away from Californian light or touch.
Our mother, canny to his latchkey nature
And his thoughtless selfishness
Smuggled two out to London;
In our rooms they stand still.

He drowned, pneumonic,
In a US hospice,
Glitter and plastic all around, quite far inland,
Which I thought was quite ironic

That Time Last Week

Like biting
Into baklava from Walworth Road & all the pastry
Bursts, splinters into layers,
Then flakes up & over your lip, into
Your mouth —
Well, it was a bit like that
At the garden last week,
When the old man sang 'Edelweiss' to his
Sad & vacant wife
& my date was late & texted me
'Sorry love, I'm messy drunk'
On an overcast 3pm on a Sunday.

But that same Sunday
I knew what acceptance was
When I saw the head gardener
In hot pink cycling shorts,
With cracked bare feet & eyes screwed up
In defiance of the gaze of others,
Reading two agonising chapters
Of a book nobody liked
To the same old man,
His wife,
To all of us.

We were okay with that,
As it seemed to keep the rainclouds at bay
& weren't the nasturtiums really
Beautiful this time of year?

(We all agreed that they were.)

A Bump In The Dark

Whilst night poured
Out into the garden
I pulled the glass doors open
& stepped through the gap
Stumbling on a stone.

A wolf spider
Raised its legs and shook them,
Angry I'd disturbed
Its little dwelling
Like a righteous old man.

A note on the process

One Night, An Elephant began as a collection of poems written by Seth over the course of the last two years, dwelling on the idiosyncrasies and uncertainties of life in an isolated London. He approached me at the beginning of this year to ask if I'd be interested in collaborating with him to turn them into a book.
I worked to translate these poems into images, to give his language a visual equivalent, a companion on the page that doesn't so much illustrate their contents as reflect them. I hope I succeeded.
-Kit

Acknoweldgments

Thanks to Eva and the team at All Around Publishing. What an unexpected joy!
Thank you Kitty, for being so patient and so talented all the time. Thank you
Eddie, for all the collections of moments and poetry, and Rosie too, for those to
come. Thanks Chris and Dot, for your clarity and your warmth. To my family,
for keeping it real. Thank you to everyone I've shared moments with, whether
they've come out as poetry or not. It's all good, all groovy.
-Seth

Thank you again to Eva and everyone at All Around for being so wonderful in
getting this project off the ground, and seeing it through to the end. To Seth, for
letting me loose on your poems and allowing the drawings to be as weird as they
wanted to be. Thank you Mamma for your guidance, and Moonboy.
-Kit